NBA CHAMPIONS BOSTON CELTICS

NBA CHAMPIONS BOSTON CELTICS

AARON FRISCH

CREATIVE EDUCATION

Published by Creative Education
P.O. Box 227, Mankato, Minnesota 56002
Creative Education is an imprint of The Creative Company
www.thecreativecompany.us

Book and cover design by Blue Design (www.bluedes.com)
Art direction by Rita Marshall
Printed by Corporate Graphics in the United States of
America

Photographs by Corbis (Steve Lipofsky), Getty Images (Brian
Babineau/NBAE, Andrew D. Bernstein/NBAE, Steve Dunwell,
Walter Iooss Jr./NBAE, Walter Iooss Jr./Sports Illustrated,
Manny Millan/Sports Illustrated, Christian Petersen, Dick
Raphael/NBAE)

Library of Congress Cataloging-in-Publication Data

Frisch, Aaron.
Boston Celtics / by Aaron Frisch.
p. cm. — (NBA champions)
Includes bibliographical references and index.
Summary: A basic introduction to the Boston Celtics
professional basketball team, including its formation in 1946,
great players such as Bill Russell, championships, and stars of
today.
ISBN 978-1-60818-131-5
1. Boston Celtics (Basketball team)—History—Juvenile
literature. I. Title.
GV885.52.B67 F75 2011
796.323'640974461—dc22   2010050559

CPSIA: 030111 PO1448

First edition
9 8 7 6 5 4 3 2 1

Cover: Rajon Rondo
Page 2: Ray Allen
Right: Jo Jo White (shooting)
Page 6: Kevin Garnett

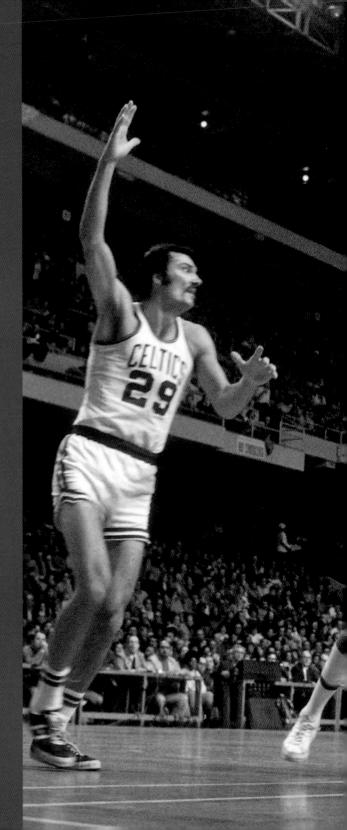

TABLE OF CONTENTS

People sometimes call Boston "Beantown" or "The Hub"

Boston is a city in Massachusetts. Boston is next to the Atlantic Ocean. It is one of the oldest cities in the United States. Boston has an **arena** called TD Garden that is the home of a basketball team called the Celtics.

The Celtics played in a famous arena called Boston Garden from 1946 to 1995

The Celtics are part of the National Basketball Association (NBA). All the teams in the NBA try to win the **NBA Finals** to become world champions. The Celtics play many games against teams called the 76ers, Knicks, Nets, and Raptors.

Red Auerbach

The Celtics started playing in 1946. They soon hired a smart coach named Red Auerbach. With Auerbach leading the team, Boston got to the **playoffs** every year in the 1950s.

SAY IT LIKE THIS

Auerbach
AR-bahk

The Celtics became the best team in the NBA in the 1960s. Boston won 11 NBA championships in 13 seasons! They beat the Los Angeles Lakers six times in the NBA Finals.

Center Robert Parish helped Boston win three championships in the 1980s

CELTICS FACTS

- Started playing: 1946

- Conference/division: Eastern Conference, Atlantic Division

- Team colors: green and white

- NBA championships:

1957 — 4 games to 3 versus St. Louis Hawks

1959 — 4 games to 0 versus Minneapolis Lakers

1960 — 4 games to 3 versus St. Louis Hawks

1961 — 4 games to 1 versus St. Louis Hawks

1962 — 4 games to 3 versus Los Angeles Lakers

1963 — 4 games to 2 versus Los Angeles Lakers

1964 — 4 games to 1 versus San Francisco Warriors

1965 — 4 games to 1 versus Los Angeles Lakers

1966 — 4 games to 3 versus Los Angeles Lakers

1968 — 4 games to 2 versus Los Angeles Lakers

1969 — 4 games to 3 versus Los Angeles Lakers

1974 — 4 games to 3 versus Milwaukee Bucks

1976 — 4 games to 2 versus Phoenix Suns

1981 — 4 games to 2 versus Houston Rockets

1984 — 4 games to 3 versus Los Angeles Lakers

1986 — 4 games to 2 versus Houston Rockets

2008 — 4 games to 2 versus Los Angeles Lakers

- NBA Web site for kids: http://www.nba.com/kids/

The Celtics playing in the 1980s (above) and Dave Cowens (opposite)

The Celtics were hard to beat for a long time. Tough center Dave Cowens helped them win the championship in 1974 and 1976. In the 1980s, the Celtics became NBA champions three more times!

Why Are They Called the Celtics?
The Celts were a group of people who used to live in Ireland and Great Britain. Many people from those countries moved to Boston. "Celtics" is a word that describes Celts.

The Celtics did not win as much in the 1990s. But in 2008, forward Paul Pierce led Boston back to the NBA Finals. The Celtics beat the Lakers to win their 17th championship. That was more than any other team had won.

In 2006, Paul Pierce scored 50 points in a single game

Celtics stars Bill Russell (above) and Bob Cousy (opposite)

wo of the Celtics' first

rs were Bob Cousy and

l Russell. Cousy was a

art guard who threw

ck passes. Russell was

ominant center. Many

ople think he was the

st defensive player ever.

SAY IT LIKE THIS

Cousy
KOO-zee

John Havlicek played for the Celtics for 16 seasons

Swingman John Havlicek came to Boston in 1962. He scored a lot of points for the Celtics. Then forward Larry Bird became the Celtics' top player. He was one of the best **sharpshooters** in the league.

SAY IT LIKE THIS

Havlicek
HAV-lih-chek

Larry Bird usually scored more than 24 points a game for Boston

In 2006, Boston added Rajon Rondo. He was a point guard who liked to race down the court at top speed. Boston fans hoped that he would help lead the Celtics to their 18th NBA championship!

Rajon Rondo used his quick hands to make many steals

GLOSSARY

arena — a large building for indoor sports events; it has many seats for fans

dominant — better than everyone else, or very hard to stop

NBA Finals — a series of games between two teams at the end of the playoffs; the first team to win four games is the champion

playoffs — games that the best teams play after a season

sharpshooters — players who are very good at making long shots

swingman — a basketball player who can play as a guard or forward

INDEX